A Pressed Leaf Keepsake Book

Fallen Leaves

Text and Images by
Louise Kollenbaum

CHRONICLE BOOKS

For Amy
And in memory of my mother
Charlotte Kollenbaum

Acknowledgments

This journal is a collaboration for which I am grateful to the following people:

The Artists

Jim Hildreth for his eye and for introducing me to digital photography; Bill Sulit for his cover collaboration and expertise in color and texture; Kathy McNicholas for her inspired calligraphy; Charles Mize for his Photoshop wizardry; Natacha González for her design and production contributions; the talented Sharon Silva for her high editorial standards; Debra Ginsberg for early research and passion; and Michael Mallery and Jim Morton at World Litho for their generosity.

The Poets

The late Maurice English, whose words have always meant so much to me; Susan Griffin for her gifts of language and friendship; Suzanne Ruby Camejo and Muldoon Elder for their language of spirit; artist-poet-scout Dee Shapiro for her countless contributions; and Beth Kephart for her inspirational book, A Slant of Sun, and her poetry.

The Friends

Deirdre English for introducing me to so much in life; the late Sue Rennert, a lover of leaves; Debra Lande of Chronicle Books for her nudge toward the simple; Tema Goodwin for that little Japanese maple that didn't quite make it; Candace Lyle Hogan and Diana Nyad for taking a moment; and Peter Allen for contributions unspoken.

The Family

Charlotte Kollenbaum, Gwen Pettus, and Amy Rennert, who are always with me; and my young scouts, Brandon Herbert, Misha Herbert, and Jacob Rennert, for their delightful perspectives.

PERMISSIONS
"Native of California" from *Bending Home: Selected and New Poems 1967-1998* © 1998 by Susan Griffin. Reprinted by permission of Copper Canyon Press, P.O. Box 271, Port Townsend, WA 98368

Printed in Hong Kong

10 9 8 7 6 5 4 3 2 1

ISBN: 0-8118-2528-0

Distributed in Canada by
Raincoast Books
8680 Cambie Street
Vancouver, B.C. V6P 6M9

CHRONICLE BOOKS
85 Second Street
San Francisco, CA 94105
www.chroniclebooks.com

Text, Design, and Illustrations: Louise Kollenbaum

Introduction

Introduction

Leaves layered on the ground, haphazardly, decomposing, melding, slowly working toward becoming one.

It's a late-summer day in the village of Colebrook, Connecticut. Its small town center is made up of only a church, a general store with part-time post office, a modest museum, and a senior center. My friends Amy and Candace are on a morning bicycle ride. The weather travels the thermometer, pleasantly warm in the sun and surprisingly cool in the shade. The leaves are already in transition, and as I walk slowly, I scan the ground, spotting colorful red-tipped maples here and there.

This isn't meant to be a leaf-gathering walk, and I am not prepared to collect. But I can't resist. Along the forest floor, my eyes struggle to distinguish the leaf from the earth, bark, berries, and twigs. The rich variety of tones and shapes seduces me. It is one of nature's best collages. The hunt is pure pleasure and the leaves I pick up are all treasures.

Later in the day, after my friends and I have joined in the local Labor Day festivities, we wander into an old, red barn-turned-shop. The proprietor sells used books, first editions and tattered volumes, books that he and his father have been collecting for decades.

The creative process begins. I search for rare book covers, dusty and worn, and place pressed leaves on their surfaces, watching them disappear into the textured patina. Hours pass. I carefully choose books with enough visual character to accompany my leaves. The idea is to try to reproduce the patterns of nature, to recapture the beauty of the forest floor.

Some of those images are pictured on these pages. They reflect memories of a special time in the country with my two best friends.

In this journal you will find suggestions for gathering, pressing, storing, and mounting leaves; stories and myths about trees and their meaning; blank pages for sketching and writing; newsprint pages for temporary storage; and translucent sleeves so that your own pressed leaves can be easily admired.

Carry this journal into your backyard, your neighborhood park, across the country, around the world. As you go, slip your collected leaves between its sheets of newsprint and record your own cherished moments on its pages.

The Life of a Tree

The reds and yellows of maples, the tawny bronze of dogwoods, the golds of oaks and sycamores, the ochre burnish of beech and birch: this is the palette of a New England autumn. For about two weeks, the countryside is painted in glorious colors, and then the leaves fall to the earth, dying so that the trees may live for another season. In spring, the process begins again.

Trees are as important to the earth's good health as the land, waters, and atmosphere are. They provide not only the basics of life—fire, furniture, food—but also great aesthetic pleasure for anyone who comes upon them. They are essential to keeping the planet's ecology in balance, supplying oxygen, preventing erosion, and providing protection from the elements.

Leaves are indispensable to the life of the tree, forming a principal link in the arboreal food chain. Although the process by which a leaf makes nourishment for the tree is simple enough to be explained in a grade-school science lesson, even botanists, beguiled by its perfect balance, consider it one of nature's miracles.

Every leaf is made up of several layers. The first, a thin, transparent sheath, allows sunlight to pass through and controls the evaporation of water. The second layer contains chlorophyll, the green pigment that holds the sunlight and converts it, along with air and water, into sugars, or food, in the process known as photosynthesis. The third layer contains ribs and veins, pipelines through which the food is moved to other parts of the tree. Beneath this transportation network is a band of loosely spaced cells that allow air to circulate and water to come in contact with carbon dioxide. Finally, the leaf's underside is home to millions of specialized pores that let carbon dioxide in and water and oxygen out.

In the warmth and light of spring and summer, the leaves work overtime to produce food for the tree. Channels in the branches, bark, and trunk become storage chambers for the excess sugars that the tree will need to survive the cold, dark winter months ahead. Sunlight turns the extra sugars stored in the leaves into pigments of various colors. These hues—golds, reds, browns, yellows—are always present within the leaves, but they become visible only with the change of the seasons, when the days become shorter and cooler. At this point, the tree prepares to rest for the winter and photosynthesis ceases.

As the green of the chlorophyll fades, the vivid colors of stored sugars emerge. Red foliage, the most brilliant paint of the autumn palette, appears only in leaves that contain certain sugars or tannins and only if the shorter days are sunny and the longer nights are quite cool.

Soon the leaves fall to the ground, where they go to work nurturing the soil and roots, continuing their indispensable contribution to the health and well-being of the tree. During the cold days of winter, the life of the tree slows to a languid pace, resting, knowing that in spring the cycle will begin again.

chapter two

E Q U I P M E N T

Getting Started

You need only a few tools for pressing leaves. A press is essential, of course, and ideally you will have a few of them. They come in many sizes and styles. Some are simple and some are quite elaborate. Some are pricey and others, for example, a big, thick, metropolitan telephone book, are free.

I own many presses but primarily use just three of them. I have a single portable lightweight wooden press for carrying along on my leaf-gathering walks. (You can use the newsprint pages at the back of this journal for transporting your collected leaves, but remember they are only temporary shelters.) In my studio I have one medium and one larger format wooden press for my works in progress.

The elements of a leaf press are standard: a wooden frame sandwiching newsprint, blotter paper, and corrugated cardboard. The frame is outfitted with straps or screws that allow the user to adjust the pressure. Before you settle on a press, however, make sure it is large enough to house both leaves and the occasional thin stem. It also should be rectangular, rather than square, to handle the broadest range of shapes and sizes.

The best press to use is the professional type that botanists employ for both leaves and flowers. Measuring twelve by eighteen inches, it is constructed of two lattice wood frames held together by straps outfitted with sturdy buckles. The lattice permits the contents to breathe, which ensures efficient drying. The buckles make adjusting the straps as leaves dry and shrink practical and easy. The press comes fully supplied with heavy blotter paper (usually one-hundred-pound stock) for absorbing excess moisture, newsprint for pressing and transporting the leaves, and cardboard. The latter, which holds the leaves between the sheets of blotter paper, has an inner fluted layer that encourages the flow of air. I find this good-sized press to be ideal. Not only can I press more leaves at one time, but I can press larger ones, too.

A visit to a craft store or an herbarium-supply store will turn up smaller field presses, usually packed with the same supplies. They are light and easy to carry, making them perfect for toting along on a walk in the woods.

If you feel comfortable in the aisles of a hardware store, you can make your own press. You'll need two same-sized pieces of quarter-inch plywood and four bolts, wingnuts, and washers. Then all you need to do is to align the two plywood pieces, fix a bolt set at each corner, and purchase the blotter paper, newsprint, and cardboard. If you lack a drill for driving the bolts through the wood, you can use nylon webbing straps to hold together the press. The dimensions of the press are up to you, but keep in mind that larger is better and that the already described professional press nicely accommodates all kinds of leaves. Big pieces of plywood can be heavy, however, so if weight is a concern, consider seeking out solidly constructed lattice to use in their place.

If talk of hardware stores and drills, herbarium-supply shops, and blotter paper seems too complicated for your initial foray into leaf pressing, start more simply with just newspapers and weights. The finished leaf will not be as flat as one done in a press, but it will be lovely. Allow several layers (up to a quarter of an inch) of paper between the pressed leaves, especially if the leaves you have gathered are quite moist.

Telephone books are another way to begin simply. Find a large one and leave lots of pages between each pressed leaf. You will need to add extra weight, too. A few bricks will do the job. Phone books are also a great way to store leaves after you have pressed them. Just be sure the pages are dry before you slip in your prized silver linden or sugar maple leaf. The disadvantage of using only a phone book is that it won't accommodate your larger pressings.

OTHER TOOLS AND MATERIALS

Once you have this journal and your permanent press, you will still need a few additional tools and supplies before you are ready to launch your pressed leaf collection.

- Newsprint, blotter paper, and cardboard, if not included with your press.

- Scissors for trimming stems and for cutting various pressing materials.

- Round-tipped tweezers for handling fragile pressed leaves.

- White glue, if you plan to mount your collection.

- X-Acto knife for trimming leaves before pressing.

chapter three

Collecting Leaves for Pressing

My mother and sister live in California's Sierra Nevada foothills—a pastoral setting. It was during one of my visits to see them that I collected my first leaves. I was initially dazzled by the smoke tree, liquid amber, and red oak. Others soon turned my head. In no time at all, I was hooked.

My early gathering days produced many surprises. Sometimes what looked to be a perfectly ordinary leaf on the ground was transformed into something extraordinary when I combined it with other discoveries in a final composition. I also found that it was a mistake to restrict myself to leaves alone. Although more difficult to press, leaves attached to stems are stunning. The subtle beauty of a lone stem, arching downward toward a single leaf, has inspired many poems—and this journal.

Feby 15

favor in regard . . . .
ity of Coke . . . .
we could know . . . my point . . . . . .
quality of a coke for . . . .
poses, for burning fire brick, for
making . . . for producing steam—
. . . . just the thing
you must have for manufacturing
. . . . of the . . . . would be going be-
yond our knowledge of the peculiar
demands you have to make on . . . .
. . . . of this kind. We . . . . only
refer you to . . . . of your
city . . . The National . . . . . . recently
formed . . . . in Cohoes . . . . .

Autumn comes to mind when one thinks of beautiful leaves, but there is no reason to limit your collecting to just those few months. Leaves are wondrous year-round.

As you set out on your search for leaves, here are a few other guidelines for successful gathering.

~ Don't leave the house without a portable field press, some newspaper, or this journal. Leaves have a way of curling or tearing by the time you reach home if you don't put them in a safe place as soon as you gather them. Good temporary storage is required at this point.

~ Try to gather leaves in the middle of the day, after any morning dew has dried and before the evening's dampness arrives.

~ Usually you are picking up leaves from the ground. Try to choose those that are dry. If they have fallen into piles, pick from the top rather than the bottom. The buried ones are certain to be damp. Mildew is a leaf's worst enemy, so the drier your selection, the longer its life.

~ Sometimes you will be captivated by a leaf still on a tree or bush. Always ask permission of the landowner before you start picking leaves. Be mindful, too, that the leaf delivers food to the tree and, unlike pinching off a flower, which actually stimulates growth, taking too many leaves is harmful.

~ Remove any visible dirt or tiny insects on the leaves. You might slip a small brush into your pocket to speed this task.

~ Try to gather leaves of a similar thickness for the same pressing. If leaves of a different thickness are on the same page, the thicker ones will prevent the thinner ones from drying properly. If you decide to press leaves of various thicknesses together, it is wise to back up your unconventional attempt with a pressing of your favorite leaves of uni-form thickness. In other words, don't be afraid to experiment, but also be careful you don't end up disappointed. This is especially important when including a stem with your leaf.

~ Selecting leaves and identifying them is a wonderful pastime. Use this journal to note the time and place you discovered each leaf and to describe or sketch the leaves, the tree, and especially the bark, which is often quite distinctive on many trees. All of this information will be helpful later when you try to establish what you have brought home. Your drawings and writings are wonderful memories for the future, too.

~ One year I received a package of freshly collected leaves from my friend Dee in Connecticut. They were gorgeous, so I displayed them in a large basket in my living room. A friend came over one afternoon and admired the colorful assortment, gently sifting through them. A few days later she discovered she had poison ivy. Be very careful when you are out gathering.

Techniques for Pressing

For most of her more than ninety-four years, my aunt Lenora has lived surrounded by flowers and trees. Whenever I visit her in the nursing home where she now resides, I bring her a small gift from nature. One time I took a bouquet of mixed flowers and a long stem from a chokecherry tree. I was drawn to the two small burgundy cherries nestled between a pair of golden leaves.

Unfortunately, Aunt Lenora promptly suffered an allergic reaction to the flowers. I hastily removed them from the room and returned with a small vase holding the lone chokecherry stem. This delighted my aunt, who said it was graceful and handsome and would always remind her of the pretty bouquet.

That night I pressed a similar stem with golden leaves and two deep red cherries to preserve the memory of our time together.

Pressing leaves is a creative endeavor, but observing a handful of rules and acting on a few tips will smooth your course.

~ Find a place where you can work without interruption and where you have plenty of room to spread out. I find music a wonderful inspiration. Put on what you like, whether it be Wagner or Ella.

~ Decide how flat you want your pressed leaves to be. If all goes well, a press will create a near-perfect leaf: flat, crisp, and with good color. Newspapers topped with weights, an easier method, will likely produce leaves with slight wrinkles and more texture. This look is wonderfully natural. Then, too, newspapers may be your only option, as it is easy to use up all the space in your presses. I suggest trying both techniques to see which look you prefer.

~ If you are using a press, place a piece of corrugated cardboard on your work surface. Top it with a sheet of blotter paper, followed by a sheet of newsprint folded in half. You will slip your leaves into the fold of the newsprint. Now place a second sheet of blotter paper on top and then a second sheet of cardboard. This "sandwich" will be used for each pressing. A word of caution: don't use a textured material, as the pattern will transfer onto the leaves.

~ Organize and edit your material as you press. Begin with thickness and variety, then think about color and geography. You may want to keep all the red and orange tones together, or create a category for multi-color leaves in transition. Or consider a geographic composition, per-

haps assembling a grouping that reflects a single afternoon of collecting on a friend's country property. When you are out gathering, resist picking up locust seeds, sycamore bark, or similar finds. These are quite thick and sometimes are three-dimensional as well, which means they should not be pressed with flat leaves. You can, however, press a leaf attached to a slim stem. The stem should be quite thin, however, as it is important to keep the height of the leaf and

stem as comparable as possible to ensure an
even pressing. If you have one or two small
berries or cherries to press, prepare for
them to fall apart between the layers of newsprint. But that is also part
of the charm, and you might even get
lucky and one will survive.

~ Select a leaf for pressing and take a close look at
it. Brush away any dirt or insects that escaped your notice
when you were out gathering, or they will forever be part of your
collection.

~ Once the leaf is ready for pressing, slip it into the fold of the
newsprint. Add more leaves if you like. This is your first sandwich.
Repeat the process, topping the first sandwich with as many more
sandwiches as you are able to assemble or will fit in your press.
Finally, cover with the top of the press and tighten the straps or bolts.

~ If you are using newspapers for pressing, allow several layers (up to
a quarter of an inch) between the leaves, especially if they are moist,
and be sure to have some good, heavy weights on hand for topping off
the stack.

~ Set the press or newspaper stack in a well-ventilated area free of moisture. Dampness is the greatest enemy of pressing, bringing on mildew
and sometimes attracting ants.

~ Successful pressings take four to eight weeks. Ideally, you should
avoid disturbing the leaves. But if you have used newspapers rather
than a press, you will probably have to change the paper. Check for
dampness by placing your hand between the sheets. If they feel cold
or moist, carefully move the leaves to a new newspaper stack. Also
check for off odors, another indication of unwanted moisture.

~ A leaf is fully dried when you can hold it by its stem and it stands
perfectly upright. Now slip the leaf into a sleeve in your journal.

As pressed leaves age, their colors fade. Some collectors become disappointed, but I love to observe the gradual muting of a brilliantly colored autumn leaf. As I watch its palette soften, I see a growing dignity that only comes with time.

A Suggested List

The leaves you gather will change during pressing and that's part of the adventure. Often I like how a leaf looks after pressing as much as how it looked when it first caught my eye.

There are a few rules. Pass up damp, wet leaves, of course. You should also avoid thick leaves and stems, waxy leaves, and leaves in clusters that create dense, overlapping layers. They are all difficult to dry.

The following list of leaves for pressing is compiled from experts, friends, and my own experience. They represent a variety of colors, shapes, and sizes. But remember, this list is only meant to be a starting point.

Experimentation is always good. Press everything that interests you. Any failures will be more than balanced by your many sucesses.

TREES

AMUR MAPLE

APPLE

BEECH

BOX ELDER

CALLERY PEAR

CANOE BIRCH

CRAB APPLE

EASTERN REDBUD

ENGLISH OAK

EUCALYPTUS

FLOWERING DOGWOOD

GINGKO

GRAY BIRCH

HAWTHORN

HORNBEAM

JAPANESE LARCH

KOUSA DOGWOOD

LIQUID AMBER

MOUNTAIN ASH

MYRTLE

NORWAY MAPLE

PEPPERIDGE

PIN OAK

PISSARD PLUM

RED MAPLE

RED OAK

SCARLET OAK

SERVICEBERRY

SILVER LINDEN

SILVER MAPLE

SMOKE TREE

SOURWOOD

SUGAR MAPLE

SWEET GUM

SYCAMORE

TAMARISK

WHITE ASH

WHITE OAK

WHITE POPLAR

WILLOW

PLANTS AND CREEPERS

ANEMONE

AZALEA

BASIL

BROOM

CLEMATIS

FERNS

HELLEBORE

HONEYSUCKLE

IVY

JASMINE

PASSION FLOWER

ROSE

SAGE

SNAKEWEED

VIRGINIA CREEPER

WANDERING JEW

Storing Your Collection

One fall I pressed so many leaves that they spilled over from my studio into the living room. Rather than apologize to visitors, I simply gave the look a designer name: "herbarium chic."

The sleeves in this journal are for displaying your favorite small- to medium-sized leaves once they are thoroughly dried. If you become a serious enthusiast, however, your collection of pressed leaves will quickly outgrow its original home. There are three good, practical methods for storing the inevitable overflow.

The first method involves acquiring as many big, old metropolitan telephone directories as you can find. They must be thick books, as they need to carry enough weight to keep the leaves perfectly flat. If you have used the books for pressing, make sure they are completely dry before recruiting them for storing your treasures. Create an archival system that works for you. For example, fill the books by season, keeping your spring discoveries separated from your autumn ones. Or you might store the leaves according to their size, color, or where they were gathered. As you fill a directory, be careful not to position the leaves too close to the spine, or they may be damaged when you close the book.

For the second method you will need stacks of old newspapers. If you have pressed your leaves using newspapers and bricks, you can store them in essentially the same way, minus the bricks. Make sure the newspapers are clean and dry. It's also a good idea to slip pieces of corrugated cardboard into the stack at several points to encourage good air circulation. When all your leaves are in place, put the newspaper stack in a big box that breathes (no solid metal or plastic) and has a cover, to keep it neat and away from the light.

Philatelists store their collections in transparent envelopes, and leaf collectors can do the same. This third method of storage is ideal if you want to determine quickly what you have already collected. Put detailed labels on the envelopes for fast and easy identification of their contents and store the envelopes in tidy stacks in closed containers to protect their contents from the light. Finding envelopes that are large enough can be a problem, however, but you can make your own if size is an issue.

No matter which method you choose for storage, always keep your pressed leaves in a dry location with good airflow. Dampness invites mildew, which will slowly destroy all your hard work. Direct sunlight and sudden temperature changes are enemies of pressed leaves, too, so keep them safe from these elements as well.

Pressed leaves are objects of beauty. Not surprisingly, collectors seldom can resist admiring their handiwork. But the leaves are also quite brittle and must be handled with considerable care. Proceed with a light touch on those occasions when you take out a pressed leaf to marvel close up at its splendor.

chapter seven

Mounting Your Pressed Leaves

*Y*ou may not be content simply to store your pressed leaves. They display such a rich spectrum of textures and colors that you will want to show off at least some of your collection. The first step to doing just that is to review some basics of mounting. Sometimes only the mounted leaves, perhaps slipped into an attractive picture frame, will be enough. Other times you will want to use your mounted specimens in more elaborate projects, such as making greeting cards or assembling a personal herbarium.

The actual mounting is not difficult, but it does take some planning and care. The tips that follow will help you maximize your creative time for the more artistic challenges that lie ahead.

$5 48

$ 17~88

$ 33~19

Nº 12 by ?

1808
June 6

May 11 by 33-19

$5 48

$ 17~88

1807 $ 33~19

~ Assemble everything you will need for mounting before you begin.

~ Stock up on sheets of 100 percent acid-free paper. Your pressed leaves will last longer if they are mounted on paper that is chemical free.

~ Select a suitable container of glue and have a small brush ready. I like plain white glue. It's inexpensive and works fine for me. Professionals use herbarium glue, however, because it doesn't break down over time. Also, some of the specialized brands permit the user to remove a glued specimen without damaging it, which is impossible with ordinary white glue.

~ Lay out your leaves in a single layer so that you can study their qualities. Then play with composition on your mounting surface until you arrive at a design that pleases you. Using a pencil, lightly map out the positions of the leaves to be sure you can re-create the placement you liked. Remember, once the glue is applied, it is usually permanent, so do your experimenting now.

~ Always apply the glue in a very thin layer. The flatter and smaller the leaf, the less glue needed. For flat leaves (achieved by using a press), use only a very thin layer of glue. For very light, thin leaves, you need only place glue on the stem. If you are working with slightly wrinkled leaves (pressed between newspapers), apply most of the glue to the stem and then lightly brush any leaf surface that is at the same height as the stem—in other words, the crest of a wrinkle—with more glue. Avoid trying to flatten the wrinkles at this stage, as the leaves are quite brittle and will crack. Also, be careful not to get any glue on your mounting surface, as most glues produce an unwanted sheen under certain light.

~ Clear contact paper with a single adhesive side is another good mounting medium. To use it, roll back the backing sheet and position the leaf on the backing. Carefully re-cover the backing with the clear paper. The leaf will stick to the paper. Now you can peel off and discard the backing and place the contact paper on your mounting sur-face, pressing it smooth. Clear contact paper is an especially good choice when you need an extra bit of surface protection for your leaves, such as when making a greeting card.

~ Thin linen tape, used by professionals to attach herbarium speci-mens, is yet another good mounting tool. Position thin strips of the tape across the stem to hold the leaf in place on the mounting surface.

~ Probably the most common destination for your mounted leaves will be a picture frame. Be sure the frame is airtight to prevent moisture from damaging your display. Also, hang the frame out of direct sunlight to prevent fading. Indeed, this sunlight rule is important for all mounted leaves, whether in frames or not.

Ideas For Pressed Leaves

*W*henever my high school biology teacher handed out a class assignment, I turned to my father, who worked in the agricultural research department at the University of California at Berkeley. He understood that while science was not my strength, art clearly was, and so he would come up with wonderful projects to work on together that combined the two.

My father would gather the materials, take the notes, and guide me with enthusiasm and patience. Skeletonizing leaves is the assignment I remember best. A skeletonized leaf is one from which the plant tissue is gone, leaving only the finely veined framework—in other words, the leaf's skeleton.

Sadly, my father's notes have not survived the years. I remember some lengthy and mysterious process, but the necessary details are now lost to me. If you search beneath deciduous trees, especially in the winter months, you can find naturally skeletonized leaves, which are usually far lovelier than their man-made counterparts. Pursuing one is a little bit like hunting down a four-leaf clover—rare, but worth the effort.

The following are projects you can undertake with your pressed leaves, along with a few organizational tips to make the creative experience a seamless one. Some of the ideas might be familiar, reminding you of days at summer camp. These are especially wonderful to do with children.

- Begin by conceptualizing your project. Try not to let logistical considerations get in the way of your dreaming. At the same time, don't come up with an idea that you can't possibly realize.

- Organize your time and space. Gather all the materials you will need before you sit down to start.

- Work out the basic aesthetic questions—size, proportion, and palette—early on. Is the composition balanced or asymmetrical, bold or simple? Are the colors the muted tones of fall or the bright hues of spring? Is the size monumental or miniature? Sketch your idea on a piece of paper. Now is the time to experiment and to change, not later when the project is already underway.

LEAF RUBBING

Leaf rubbings are simple and fun and a good place to begin. Place the leaf on a surface where it won't slip once you begin to rub it. Position a sheet of very thin paper over the leaf and gently rub steadily across it with a crayon or piece of charcoal. (You will need to hold the tool lengthwise and parallel to the paper.) The patterns of the leaf will slowly emerge in relief on the paper. When I was a child, I used crayons for rubbings. Now I experiment to find out what effects I can achieve with various charcoals, pastels, even pencil. Art-supply stores will sell single sticks in a variety of materials and colors.

Leaf Silhouette

Arrange a single leaf or a pattern of leaves on a sheet of paper. Dip a toothbrush into a small container of water-based paint and move your finger quickly across the bristles or firmly strike the handle of the brush, spraying the page with paint. Wait until the paint is almost dry and repeat the process until the entire page is well covered with spatters. Let dry, then remove the leaf or leaves to reveal a silhouette.

Waxed-Paper Leaf Hanging

On an ironing board, place a leaf between two sheets of waxed paper. Cover the paper with a soft, thin towel. Set the iron on medium heat and iron the leaf for a minute or two. The heat secures the leaf inside the waxed paper, sealing it and preserving it at the same time. Trim to the desired shape and suspend the leaf panel from a length of ribbon or twine in a place where indirect sunlight will stream through it.

Rice Paper Leaf Hanging

Roll back the backing from a sheet of opaque contact paper. Position the leaf on the contact paper and discard the backing. Place a piece of transparent rice paper over the leaf and press it smooth, adhering it firmly to the contact paper. Trim to the desired shape and slip into a frame. Hang or stand the frame where indirect light will shine through the opaque side.

NOTEPAPER AND NOTE CARD

To make one-of-a-kind notepaper, place a small spot of white glue on the back of a leaf and adhere it inside a folded sheet of writing paper. Or purchase blank greeting cards and decorate them with leaves, adding your own message at the same time. For an even simpler but still memorable card, tuck a single loose leaf into the fold.

GIFT TAG

Adhere small, colorful leaves to clear contact paper (to protect the leaves) and then attach the contact paper to cardstock to make gift tags.

DINING TABLE CENTERPIECE

Display fall leaves as a centerpiece for your dining table. Create a horizontally shaped mound, tapering the leaves at either end. Place the more colorful leaves where they are the most visible and keep them distant from one another. Fill in the spaces with the less showy leaves.

PLACE SETTING DECORATION

To dress up the place settings for a special harvest meal, put a single pressed leaf on each dinner plate.

HERBARIUM

Put together your own herbarium from leaves in your collection. Using glue, mount the leaves on a poster-sized sheet of heavyweight, acid-free paper. Arrange them much as you would if you were pressing them but with an eye toward composition. Be careful not to crowd them. To imitate the style of a professional herbarium, place pieces of thin linen tape across the stems. Label each leaf with both its common and Latin names, where you found it, and the date. Frame the arrangement for hanging.

Trees and Their Meanings

The symbolic meanings associated with trees and their leaves vary from culture to culture and era to era. The following is a list of some common trees and their symbolic significance as revealed in history, myth, and legend.

ACACIA: The acacia symbolized chaste love to the North American Indians, who used its wood for making their bows and its thorns for making their arrows.

ALDER: Traditionally used for building bridges because of its resistance to water rot and long associated with oracular powers, the alder represented protection and wisdom to the Celts.

ALMOND: The almond tree, prized as a source of perfume, medicine, and food, symbolized purity to the Victorians.

APPLE: Perhaps the earliest cultivated tree, the apple tree yields the famed fruit of temptation and is symbolic of the giving of love.

ASH: In Norse mythology, the first man was created from an ash (and the first woman from an elm). An ash leaf nearly always has an odd number of leaflets, so that someone who finds a leaf with an even number is considered as lucky as someone who finds a four-leaf clover.

AVOCADO: Mayan, Incan, and Aztecan mothers believed that the avocado carried medicine to cure every ill; thus, the tree came to represent healing.

BEECH: The early European books were fashioned from thin pieces of the wood of the beech, a tree that came to symbolize knowledge and wisdom.

BIRCH: The Celts associated the birch with fertility and protection and thus traditionally fashioned their baby cradles from it.

CEDAR: The Victorians held the cedar tree in high esteem, declaring it a symbol of incorruptibility and fidelity.

CHESTNUT: Because of its bountiful harvest, the chestnut tree symbolized luxury to the Victorians.

CYPRESS: A symbol of sorrow, cypress was traditionally used by medieval Europeans for building coffins.

DOGWOOD: Known as Apollo's tree in Greek mythology, the dogwood, which flourishes where many other trees perish, came to be a symbol of durability.

ELDER: Associated with a variety of female household gods in Celtic culture, the elder also yielded the material used for making Celtic witches' sticks.

ELM: In ancient Greece, the elm was associated with death and rebirth.

EUCALPYTUS: Because the leaves of the eucalyptus have long been used to make powerful medicines, the tree is widely associated with healing.

FIG: The fig tree is traditionally a symbol of knowledge. In the Garden of Eden, Adam and Eve were said to have covered themselves with its leaves after eating its sweet fruits.

FIR: The Celts saw the remarkable height of the majestic fir as a symbol of foresight.

HAWTHORN: The hawthorn carries both delicate flowers and sharp thorns, making it a symbol of both hope and bad luck to the Victorians.

HAZEL: Baskets and other containers made from hazel wood were thought by the Celts to provide wisdom and poetic inspiration.

HOLLY: The holly tree symbolized immortality to the ancient mystics, and it was believed that a man who carried a holly leaf in his pocket became immediately attractive to women.

JUNIPER: A symbol of asylum to the Celts, the juniper was also believed to protect against witchcraft.

LARCH: In Siberian mythology, the first man was created from a larch (and the first woman from a fir).

LAUREL: The ancient Romans wore laurel wreaths to symbolize victory and achievement.

LINDEN: The tall, beautiful linden tree symbolized conjugal love to the Victorians.

MANGO: The mango tree is a symbol of immortality in many Asian cultures.

MAPLE: In Native American lore, the spreading maple represents success and abundance.

OAK: A symbol of strength in many cultures, the oak in Greek mythology is associated with Zeus, the most powerful of all the gods.

OLIVE: The olive branch is universally associated with peace.

POPLAR: The poplar was long ago nicknamed the whispering tree. According to legend, Christ's cross was fashioned from its branches, and its leaves continue to quiver constantly in remembrance.

ROWAN: Revered by the Celts, the rowan was believed to protect against enchantment.

SYCAMORE: The erect, many-branched sycamore represented curiosity to the Victorians.

WALNUT: Prized for its rich brown wood and sweet, oily kernels, the walnut symbolized intellect to the Victorians.

WILLOW: A grand tree with downward-curving branches, the willow has long symbolized sorrow in the West.

YEW: Early Christians saw the yew as sacred and often constructed their places of worship and places of burial near the tall, stately trees.

chapter ten

GLOSSARY

A Glossary of Common Terms

My art school professor's favorite location for our drawing class was the botanical gardens. When we first started going there, my instinct was to begin drawing at the focal point, the colorful, showy leaf or flower. From there I would work backward, retracing the origins of growth down the stem into a complicated web, putting the greater challenge at the end of my task rather than at the beginning. I eventually learned to start at the base and to study and understand the construction of growth, working out the composition in detail from the bottom up.

This new awareness encouraged me to study some basic botanical terminology, which also may be of help to you as you go about collecting and pressing your leaves. What follows is a selection of the most commonly used words in the scientific world of trees.

ANNUAL: A plant that completes its life cycle in one growing season.

ARBORICULTURE: The cultivation of trees and shrubs.

AXIL: The inner angle between a leaf and its stem.

BIENNIAL: A plant that completes its life cycle in two growing seasons.

BLADE: The thin, flat expanded part of a leaf.

BLEED: To lose sap through a wound.

BLOSSOM: The flower of a plant.

BONSAI: The art of growing trained, dwarfed trees or plants in containers to achieve a miniature landscape.

CAMBIUM: A tree's thin inner sheath, between the sapwood and the inner bark, that manufactures cells and gives rise to secondary growth.

CANOPY: The area of the tree measured by the farthest reaches of its branches.

CATKIN: A slender, drooping flower cluster.

CHLOROSIS: A condition in green plants due to their failure to obtain iron, resulting in yellowing leaves.

COLLAR: The point at which the main branch of a tree meets the trunk.

COMPOUND LEAF: A leaf that has fully separated parts, or blades.

CONIFER: Evergreen tree or shrub bearing seeds in cones.

COPPICE: A thicket of small trees.

CORM: A thickened underground stem.

CROWN: The entire branch structure, including leaves and twigs, at the top of a tree.

DECIDUOUS: A tree or plant that sheds all of its leaves and remains leafless during the same season each year.

DEFOLIATION: The unnatural and detrimental loss of a plant's leaves.

DENDROCHRONOLOGY: The science of dating event and cyclic weather patterns by studying growth rings in trees.

DIGITATE LEAF: A leaf in which the leaflets all grow at the same point from the stem.

EVERGREEN: A plant or tree than never loses all of its leaves throughout a full growing season.

FAMILY: A group of related plants.

FROND: A large leaf with many divisions, such as a fern or palm.

GENUS: The smallest natural group containing related but distinct species. The first word of a plant name.

HEARTWOOD: The older, harder, nonliving central core of a tree.

LEAFLET: A division or blade of a compound leaf.

NODE: The place on a shoot where leaves or flowers originate.

PALISADE LAYER: The part of the leaf containing chlorophyll.

PERENNIAL: Flowering, nonwoody plant that lives for more than two years.

PETIOLE: The stalk of a leaf.

PHLOEM: A moist sleeve located beneath the main bark of a tree that carries food from the leaves to the rest of the tree.

PINNATE LEAF: A leaf in which the leaflets grow along the sides of the stem.

RHIZOME: A thickened underground, usually horizontal, stem.

RIBS: Part of the framework of a leaf that, along with the smaller veins, holds it open to sunlight and air and helps transport food to the rest of the plant.

RIND: The tough outer bark of a tree or shrub.

SAP: The fluid of a plant.

SAPLING: A young tree that measures not more than four inches in diameter at breast height.

SAPWOOD: The younger, softer, living layer of wood that lies between the cambium and the heartwood and carries water and minerals from the roots to the leaves.

SIMPLE LEAF: A leaf in which the blade is a single piece.

SPECIES: The basic unit of classification of plants. The second word of a plant name.

SPORE: A reproductive cell capable of producing a new plant.

SPUR: A small side twig that often bears a cluster of leaves.

STIPULES: Pairs of leaflike appendages found at the base of certain leaves.

STOLON: A shoot that trails along the surface of the ground.

STOMATA: Valvelike cells on the bottom skin of the leaf that act as breathing pores.

TAPROOT: The main root of a tree that grows vertically downward.

TENDRILS: Spiraling, threadlike projections that enable some vines to climb a trellis or other support.

TOPIARY: The technique of training or cutting trees and shrubs into ornamental shapes.

TUBER: The thickened portion of an underground stem from which the plant grows.

VARIEGATED: A leaf irregularly patterned with various colors.

WHORL: The arrangement of three or more structures—leaves, branches, blossoms—at one joint on a trunk or stem.

WOODY: Describes a plant possessing hard tissues that will retain their shape long after death.

WOUND: The mark left on a tree after a branch is removed.

You should go to a pear tree for pears,
not to an elm.

- PUBLILIUS SYRUS

In her last
hours they moved her
to the other side
of the building
and from there
she could see
a plum tree
past its bloom and bearing
but still
with the wine-dark leaves.

- SUSAN GRIFFIN

Against the blue stands
A pine tree etched
By tonight's noon.
                    - RANSETSU

Russet Leaves
Amidst this swirl of colors
our lives convene and touch
and kiss and pass as if by
chance:
And no one knows how
ends the dance . . .
- SUZANNE CAMEJO AND MULDOON ELDER

I think that I shall never see
A poem lovely as a tree.
- Joyce Kilmer

Pines, black backdrops
for russet and ochre oaks.

Maple sigh saffron yellow-
A flash of sumac fire.

In the breeze
trees race to undress
a dance of veils.

Leaves flutter down in spirals.
Unfolding thoughts
mimic the descent.

- DEE SHAPIRO

If poetry comes not as naturally as the Leaves to
a tree it had better not come at all.

- JOHN KEATS

Who has seen the wind?
Neither you nor I:
But when the trees bow down their heads,
The wind is passing by.
- CHRISTINA GEORGINA ROSSETTI

Woodman, spare that tree!
Touch not a single bough!
In youth it sheltered me,
And I'll protect it now.
- GEORGE POPE MORRIS

Dearer than all anatomies of thought
Stand up, as ultimate and fair,
These shapes of brightness, to no ending wrought,
But sinuous flowing out of stainless air.
- MAURICE ENGLISH

You cannot see the wood for the trees.
- JOHN HEYWOOD

I had worried about the Japanese maple
That had lasted
The late winter mewl and the burn of the moonlight
And the child riding its limb
Like a buoy. Nothing
Could survive all that, I said, nothing,
And then survive its own
Fecundity, too, its own hard-candy
Buds, its bursts of helicoptering seeds, the blameless
Beauty of its leaves.

- BETH KEPHART

Keep a green tree in your heart and
perhaps the singing bird will come.
- CHINESE PROVERB